THE SOLDIER THROUGH THE AGES

THE ROMAN LEGIONARY

Martin Windrow

Illustrated by
·Gerry Embleton

Franklin Watts
London   New York   Toronto   Sydney

First published in Great Britain in 1984 by
Franklin Watts Ltd
12a Golden Square
London W1

First published in the USA by
Franklin Watts Inc.
387 Park Avenue South
New York
N.Y. 10016

First published in Australia by
Franklin Watts Australia
I Campbell Street
Artarmon
NSW 2064

UK edition ISBN: 0 86313 155 7
US edition ISBN: 0-531-03781-9
Library of Congress Catalog Card No: 84-50019

Designed by James Marks

Printed in Belgium

Contents

Guardians of the frontier

The Roman empire was probably the greatest in the history of the world – the biggest, richest, best organized and longest lasting. Between about 200 BC and AD 200 it spread from its Italian heartland across all Western Europe, the Balkans, the lands around the Mediterranean, North Africa, the Middle East and even part of what is now the USSR.

Not everyone who lived in the empire was a Roman citizen. Three main kinds of people owed obedience to the emperor: citizens; free people who did not have rights of citizenship; and slaves. In the early empire, the citizens were those whose

◁ A legionary patrols a stretch of the eastern Roman frontier in Germany, some time in the 2nd century. Frontier defenses were not usually continuous walls but lightly held lines of watchtowers which gave warning of attack to forts further inside the empire.

▷ The Roman empire in the 2nd century AD. At one time the eastern "corridor" reached the Caspian Sea. This vast area was guarded by about 28 legions – some 160,000 legionaries – plus some 220,000 auxiliary troops in other types of units.

families originally came from Italy. As time passed, citizenship was granted to other classes. From the 3rd century AD anyone who was not a slave was a citizen. But before this happened, it was a great advantage to be a citizen. Citizens had special rights relating to the law and taxation; and only citizens could do certain types of government jobs. One such was to serve in the regular army.

The army that won the Roman empire, and guarded it for 600 years, was unlike any other of its day. And the heart of its strength was the legionary – the citizen volunteer serving in one of the permanent brigades or legions. The legionary was a very modern sort of soldier. He was a full-time professional who enlisted for a set period, usually 25 years. He might live anywhere in the empire; but as long as he was a Roman citizen he could join an army that was organized in the same way all across the huge expanse of empire. He and his comrades spoke the same language; wore the same uniforms; carried the same weapons, and used them in the same way; lived in the same sort of forts; earned the same pay; were promoted through the same ranks; and obeyed the same regulations.

A soldier's oath

A young man who wanted to enlist as a soldier would get himself a letter of introduction from someone who knew an army officer. Then he reported for an interview at the local army headquarters. A doctor examined him to make sure he was fit and healthy and at least 5 ft 8 in (1.78 m) tall. An officer questioned him to make sure he was a genuine citizen, and not a runaway slave, a criminal or a foreigner. If he passed these interviews, the recruit was allowed to take the army oath.

After an impressive ceremony the new soldier was given a cash bonus of four months' pay. Then he was sent, together with other new legionaries, to join his unit.

When the recruit arrived, his particulars were taken down by an officer of his century, or 80-man company. Six centuries made a cohort, a battalion of about 480 men. Officers called centurions commanded both centuries and cohorts; this rank had several different grades. Ten cohorts made up a legion, a brigade of about 5,000 men. Each legion had a name and number. The name usually referred to the place where it was formed, or to the emperor then reigning, or to a nickname won in battle. *Legio IX Hispana*, for example was the "9th Legion, raised in Spain," and *Legio XII Fulminata* the "12th Legion, the Thunderbolts."

▷Inside the great hall of the legion's headquarters building, recruits take the army oath. They stand before the chapel which houses the pay-chest, altars to the gods and the unit's sacred standards. These images mounted on poles were regarded like a modern regiment's flag. They were the symbols of the unit's pride, and were respected almost as religious relics. The oath bound the soldiers to be brave, obedient, honest and loyal at all times.

△Each legion had one
eagle, its sacred battle-
standard (center); and
another standard with its
own badge.

From civilian to legionary

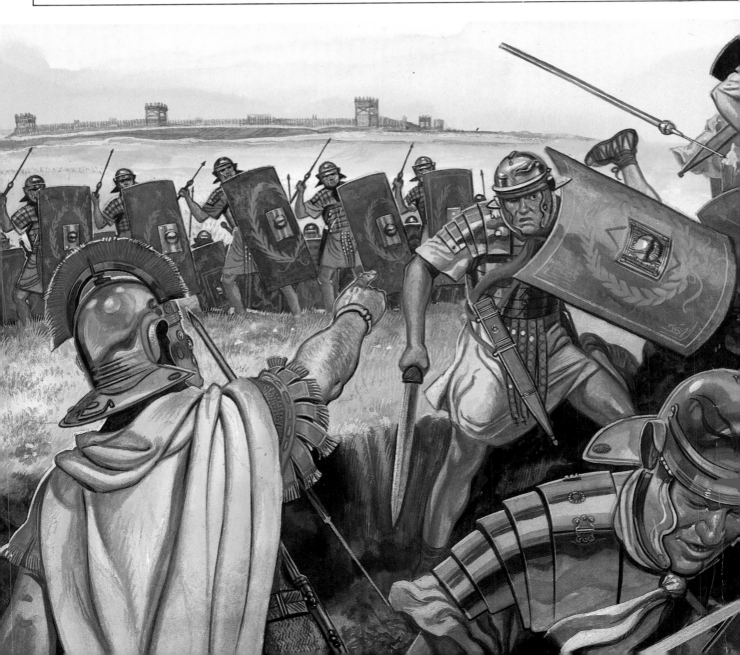

The new recruit must have found life strange and uncomfortable during his first few months of basic training. It was probably his first time away from home. He lived in a long barracks, which was divided up into small rooms by partitions. Eight men shared a small bedroom and a lobby where they kept their gear.

The new legionary was made to march and run long distances and to practice carrying a heavy pack. He spent hours doing the long-jump and high-jump and vaulting a wooden horse to make him strong and agile. Before long he had to repeat these exercises wearing full armor. If there was water nearby, he was taught to swim. He learned to pile his equipment on his shield and carry it on his head when fording rivers.

While this physical training continued, he was taught drill movements on the parade ground. In battle the Romans fought in disciplined ranks, so it was important for the men to learn how to move neatly from one formation to another at the sound of different trumpet calls. Eventually long hours of practice made these maneuvers second nature.

◁ **Top** Recruits spent hours each day learning how to handle their weapons. At first they practiced against wooden posts set in the ground. Later, they were paired off to fight each other in mock battles. They were given dummy wooden swords and javelins, and wicker shields, all weighted so that they were twice as heavy as the real thing.

◁ The legionaries were also trained for war by practicing attacks on the ramparts of dummy forts, scrambling over steep banks and fences in full gear, chased by bellowing instructors.

The tools of war

In the early years of the Roman empire, soldiers wore shirts of ring-mail. These were flexible and allowed easy movement, which is vital in hand-to-hand fighting. But they were also heavy and tiring to wear. Ring-mail gave good protection against cutting weapons, but a hard blow with a sharp-pointed spear or arrow could burst through the rings.

In about AD 40 a new sort of armor appeared. It was cleverly made of overlapping iron plates fixed to a harness of leather straps. The curved plates overlapped at the edges, so that the soldier could still move and bend easily. This armor was surprisingly light, and it could be folded up to fit into the soldier's pack.

The helmet usually worn with the ring-mail was a simple bronze type shaped like a back-to-front jockey cap. With the new plate armor came a much smarter and more efficient iron helmet, which gave better protection. Its neck-piece was curved down and around, and its cheek-plates covered more of the face.

The soldier also carried a big shield, curved to fit around his body. It was made of plywood, with metal edges and central boss.

The soldier's weapons were two javelins – one heavy and one light – and a short stabbing-sword. The sword was slung on the right side. No one knows exactly how the legionary drew it from this awkward position. He also carried a dagger slung on a belt decorated with metal plates. An apron of weighted straps hung down from the belt to protect his groin.

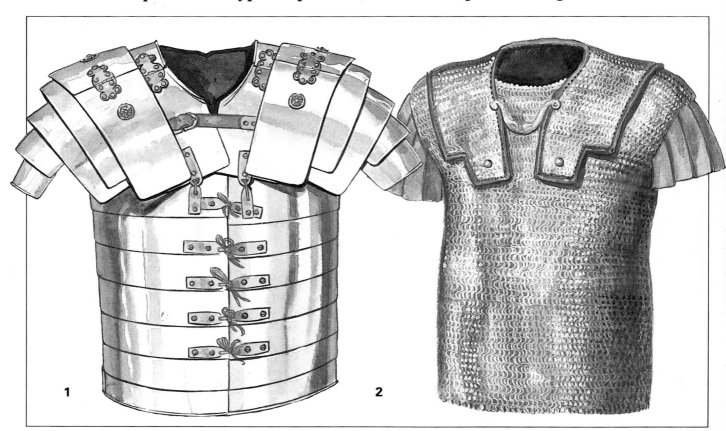

1

2

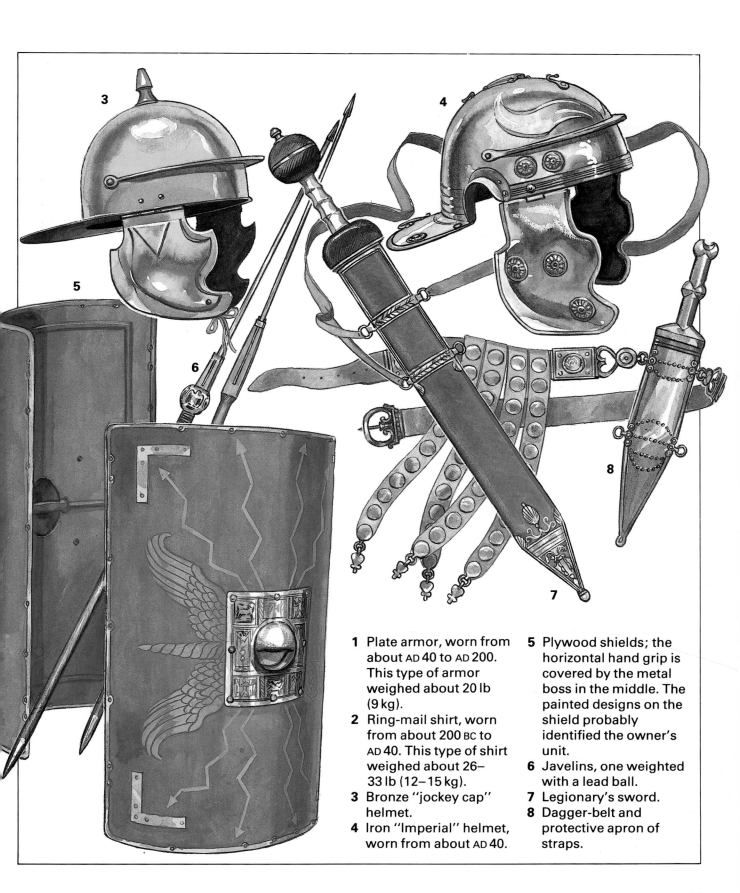

1 Plate armor, worn from about AD 40 to AD 200. This type of armor weighed about 20 lb (9 kg).

2 Ring-mail shirt, worn from about 200 BC to AD 40. This type of shirt weighed about 26–33 lb (12–15 kg).

3 Bronze "jockey cap" helmet.

4 Iron "Imperial" helmet, worn from about AD 40.

5 Plywood shields; the horizontal hand grip is covered by the metal boss in the middle. The painted designs on the shield probably identified the owner's unit.

6 Javelins, one weighted with a lead ball.

7 Legionary's sword.

8 Dagger-belt and protective apron of straps.

On the march

No matter how well armed and trained the Roman soldier was, he was only useful if his commanders could bring him to the battlefield when and where he was needed. To move the legions quickly, the army built a superb network of straight, stone-paved roads linking their towns and fortresses. There were no transport wagons for the legionary: he marched everywhere in his famous hob-nailed sandals.

Even in peacetime a soldier did about three marches a month. He had to march 20 Roman miles (nearly 30 km) in five hours and then, at the end, help build a defended camp. He had to be fit enough to work, or fight, after his journey.

The marching legionary wore full armor, but unless the enemy was close by he carried his helmet and shield slung by straps. Over his shoulder he carried his two javelins, as well as a forked or T-shaped pole on which he tied his personal gear and rations.

Each squad of eight legionaries shared a baggage mule which carried their leather tent and other heavy or awkward items of camping equipment. There were probably extra rations too: when the army was on campaign in enemy country the soldiers had up to three weeks' food. On the march the food was probably plain: grain for making hard biscuit-bread; vegetables like onions and dried beans, which kept a long time; and perhaps a little dried fish or meat. The usual drink was a sour wine.

In hostile territory the column of men was arranged for the march in a special order. Cavalry guarded the flanks from ambush; and the commanders, baggage and heavy equipment were placed in the middle, guarded by fighting units in front and behind.

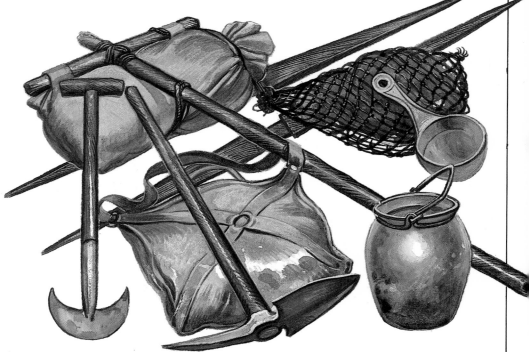

▷ **The legionary's load**
A leather sack and a satchel with cross-straps held cloak, spare clothes and sandals, personal belongings and tools. Each man had a bronze, ladle-shaped mess-kit and a cooking pot or bucket. The net bag was probably for food. Everyone had emergency rations for three days – usually thick biscuits of hard-baked wheat bread, with perhaps some beans, lentils, onions or dried fish. Two wooden stakes, for making the fence around each night's camp, were also carried.

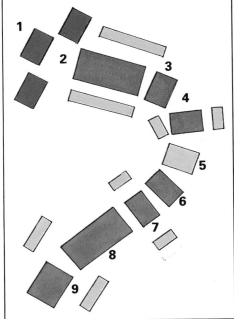

△ Marching column in enemy territory:
1 Advance guard, auxiliary infantry.
2 Legionaries, cavalry flank guards.
3 Engineers.
4 Senior commanders, cavalry flank guards.
5 Cavalry.
6 Catapults.
7 Junior commanders, cavalry flank guards.
8 Legionaries.
9 Rearguard infantry and cavalry.

◁ The legionary's marching gear probably weighed about 40 lb (18 kg) in all – the equivalent of carrying a medium-sized television set on his shoulders for 20 miles (30 km)! But the load was probably quite comfortable if properly balanced – after all, modern bricklayers still use a similar hod for carrying stacks of bricks.

The price of a peaceful night

In country where there was the slightest risk of attack, the legionary had to help dig an entrenched camp at the end of his day's march. A surprise night attack was always dangerous, but this sensible precaution cut down the risk of the camp being overrun.

Surveyors traveled ahead of the column to choose a campsite before the troops arrived. A good place was one that was situated near water, on level ground and not overlooked by hills or woods. The surveyors laid out the plan of the camp with pegs and flags. Within the camp, each group of tents was placed in the same position every night. This made the job of pitching camp quicker and easier. It also helped the soldiers to find their way around after dark, which was vital if they were attacked.

When the main column arrived, half the troops took up position to guard the other half, who worked. The men assigned to dig the defenses stacked their spears, shields and helmets and set to work. This familiar job probably took no more than a couple of hours.

△Roman tools: semi-circular turf cutter, pickaxe and mattock, which combined a pick and a broad blade.

▷Legionaries making a night camp. First they cut and stacked a wide strip of turf. Then they dug a trench, about 9 ft 9 in (3 m) deep by 13 ft (4 m) wide at the top. The earth was piled into a rampart 4 ft (1.25 m) high, and faced with a wall of the cut turf. The wooden stakes which each man carried were then stuck along the top of the rampart and tied together to make a fence.

The men were issued with picks, mattocks, baskets and saws. They must have had shovels as well, probably carried with the unit's baggage. Each man had a short chain to use when carrying stacks of turf.

△A Roman camp was shaped like a playing card, with round corners. It had four gates and three main roads. The headquarters tents were set up at the junction of two roads, and the other tents were positioned in lines on each side.

Duty under the centurion's eye

The legionary spent far more of his life laboring than fighting. In peacetime his centurions gave him no chance to become idle! The legionary was the all-purpose workman of the empire: building roads, draining marshes, putting up aqueducts and bridges, quarrying stone and making tiles for every kind of public building. The timber used for most temporary military buildings and fort stockades needed replacing about every ten years – and it was the legionary who got the job. He probably preferred another of his regular duties, which was to act as a policeman or customs officer in small detachments scattered around the countryside.

Even in fort garrisons there was plenty to do each day. Simply polishing iron armor free of rust took the legionary hours each week. And the centurions could always find him other jobs – sweeping, digging, chopping, repairing, loading, carrying, in addition to guard duties. Nor did the Roman soldier have weekends off – although he seems to have had regular free days for the many religious holidays.

▷A gang of soldiers repair a barracks, watched by their centurion. His uniform is more elaborate than theirs. His vine-wood stick was not only a badge of rank – as slow soldiers found out painfully! Centurions were the backbone of the army – the professional officers who led companies and battalions in battle, and kept men busy and disciplined in peacetime. Harsh taskmasters, they often demanded bribes to let men off the worst "fatigues." The only permanent escape was a special job such as a clerk, smith or cobbler.

Engineers and artillery

A Roman army on campaign usually took siege-machines to help capture enemy towns and forts. Roman engineers were skilled and patient: a siege might last for months, but the Romans nearly always won in the end.

Before attacking a defended stronghold, the Romans often built their own belt of walls and trenches all round it, to stop help reaching the garrison. Then they made ramps of logs and earth across the enemy's defensive ditch. These allowed them to push their siege-machines against the walls. The usual machines were battering rams, to knock walls down, and towers, which acted as giant protected ladders for the legionaries to climb to the top of the walls. Sometimes as tall as 100 ft (about 30 m), the towers had drawbridges at the top to carry the Roman troops across on to the enemy rampart.

These machines were built on the spot: skilled legionary craftsmen could make most of the equipment an army needed. The outer surfaces of the machines were protected by padding, metal plates and wet hides against stones and fire-arrows shot by the enemy.

In battles and sieges the Roman legionary was supported by his "artillery" – that is, by catapults throwing stones or heavy arrows. Each legion had 60 catapults. They ranged in size from small machines which were carried on mule-carts to huge siege catapults the size of cranes.

The small catapults threw stones about the size of an orange, or heavy arrows with wooden "feathers." These were surprisingly accurate, and could hit a man at about 180 yd (165 m). Against close-packed enemies they were deadly up to about 480 yd (440 m). The big siege catapults threw stones weighing about 100 lb (45 kg), to shake down city walls.

▽Small stone- and arrow-throwing catapults were made of wood with metal fittings. Twisted ropes of animal sinew acted like springs. The crew wound the cord back with a windlass, then released a catch, which allowed the cord to fly forward, hurling the stone or arrow out.

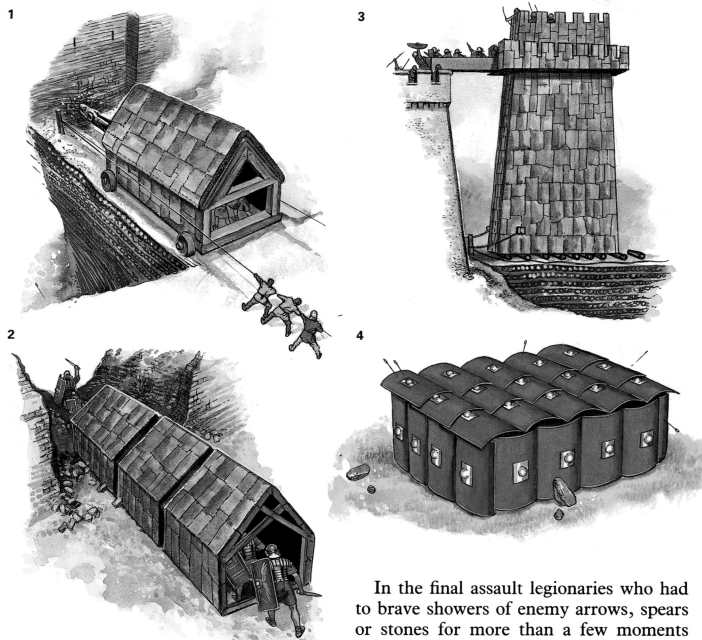

1 Battering rams hung on ropes inside wheeled "huts" which protected the men swinging the heavy, iron-shod beams.

2 Similar huts, arranged in tunnels, protected assault troops charging up to the broken walls.

3 Siege towers had space for archers and small catapults, giving covering fire to the men.

4 It is said that the "tortoise" formation was strong enough for a chariot to drive across the top!

In the final assault legionaries who had to brave showers of enemy arrows, spears or stones for more than a few moments were ordered into "tortoise" formation. They held their shields above their heads, making an interlocking roof. Meanwhile, men at the edges of the formation made "walls" with their shields. This moving "box" protected the legionaries from missiles until they were close enough to the enemy to open out again into fighting ranks.

Many races, one army

△On completing 25 years' service, each auxiliary was given a bronze diploma instead of the cash bonus the legionary received. The diploma recorded his service, and proved that he and his descendants had earned citizenship.

A Roman army on campaign included not just the heavy legionary infantry but also strong auxiliary units of cavalry and light infantry. These auxiliaries were recruited in frontier areas, among people not yet awarded citizenship. An auxiliary's career was as long and hard as a legionary's, and much worse paid; but after serving his time, he was granted citizenship for himself and his descendants.

Auxiliaries served under Roman commanders in separate cohorts, never in complete legions. They usually garrisoned forts on distant frontiers, far from their homes. Syrian archers, Balkan cavalry and Iraqi boatmen served in Britain; and British auxiliaries fought in Rumania and Morocco.

An army camp on active service was a lively mixture of men from different races, all serving the same cause. Some rivalry was natural, but generally they got along well. It was useful for commanders to have a choice of soldiers with different skills and weapons, who could do different tasks on the battlefield.

◁Legionaries chat around the camp-fires with auxiliaries wearing different uniforms and armor. Auxiliaries often had more old-fashioned equipment, such as bronze helmets and ring-mail. Sometimes they kept the types of costume and weapon traditional in their part of the world, and their shields were usually oval. All Roman cavalry units were auxiliaries.

Battle tactics

The key to Roman success was discipline. It made the legionary almost unbeatable in a pitched battle on open ground. The Romans fought together in tight formation, using familiar drills and obeying trumpet signals. Their enemies – usually strong, brave tribesmen – fought as individuals.

The warriors were seldom as well equipped as the legionaries. Apart from a few chiefs, they did not wear armor, and their weapons were often unsuited for fighting men in iron helmets and breastplates.

The Romans began their attacks with volleys of javelins. Even if the javelins stuck in the warriors' shields, they still did damage. The javelin necks were of soft iron, which bent on impact. They could not be pulled out and thrown back, and stuck in the shield they made it too heavy and awkward to carry.

After throwing their javelins, the Romans closed in to fight with shield and sword. They used their big shields to knock their enemies off balance. Then they stabbed with their short swords around the edge of their shields, up into the warrior's unprotected body.

▷ Ranks of legionaries move into the attack against Celtic warriors, such as they met in Gaul and Britain. In ranks six or eight men deep, the Romans make an almost solid wall with their shields. If one falls, his comrade behind steps forward to keep the line intact. Few tribal armies could resist these military skills for long, especially since tribal warriors had not learned how to fight together in obedience to drills and orders.

Command and control

A Roman general, commanding one or more legions and perhaps a dozen or more auxiliary cohorts, did not lead his men into the attack in person. In the heat of battle he would have been just one more swordsman – and a rather elderly and out-of-breath swordsman too! Instead he took up a position, usually on some convenient hilltop, which gave him a good view of everything that happened. He could watch how his plans were succeeding and give orders to move his cohorts, auxiliaries and catapults about the battlefield as he thought best. Each legion had 120 cavalrymen permanently attached, and one of their main duties was carrying messages for the commanders. Massed trumpeters could also signal the simpler orders by blowing calls which soldiers had been trained to recognize.

▽ A general, surrounded by his staff officers, his standard-bearers and trumpeters to blow signals. A mounted courier is being given a message for a cohort commander. Reserves of fresh troops wait nearby in case they are needed.

▷ The legionary's attacking drill. First he threw his light javelin, which had longer range. Then he moved closer and threw his heavy javelin. Finally he charged at his enemy with sword drawn and shield held up.

▷Legionaries and whole units were trained to replace one another in battle when they became tired. They fought in solid ranks, but could open gaps in the ranks when ordered. On the signal, fresh second-rank men (**1**) moved forward into gaps, while tired front-rank men (**2**) moved back; both ranks then closed the gaps again. (**3**) Units could move right back and form a new rear rank while resting. If the enemy broke through the front rank, the "saw" maneuver (**4**) by units in the second rank soon dealt with them.

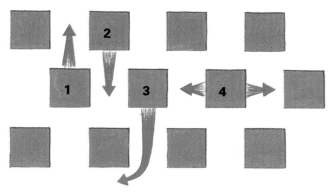

The general always held back a reserve of troops for emergencies. Even if he had only one legion, he kept at least one cohort – often, the senior and most experienced 1st Cohort – close to his command post. Units of auxiliary cavalry were also held ready for his orders. As he watched the way the battle developed, the general could send them into action at the right moment and in the right place. He always had fresh troops ready to stop an enemy breakthrough or to reinforce his own units at the enemy's weak point. Through study of the history of previous wars, Roman officers learned in advance all the things which were likely to go wrong in the heat of action, and what steps to take to cope with emergencies.

Risks and rewards

The soldier's life was always dangerous, and his excellent armor and training could not entirely protect the legionary from wounds. Even in peacetime, accidents must have been common, for soldiers spent much of their time in heavy laboring work. Although the Romans did not understand all the causes of infection, and often died young from injuries or illnesses which can be treated today, they did their best to look after their soldiers.

Many forts had hospitals, and all units had medical officers and medical orderlies trained in first aid. Broken bones were set, arrowheads removed, and wounds sewn up. In serious cases limbs were amputated. Treatment without proper anesthetics must have been a horrible ordeal. No doubt many men died from shock or infection after operations. Some herbal drugs and ointments were known, however, and these were probably quite effective for minor problems.

If he risked wounds and disease, the legionary could also hope for the good luck of rewards and decorations. Keen and skillful soldiers were promoted; there were three junior officers' posts in each 80-man century, which brought in half as much pay again as a legionary received. If the soldier was promoted to centurion, he enjoyed a big pay increase, an easier life, and interesting jobs both inside the legion and away from it.

Bravery in battle was rewarded by decorations. Soldiers were given special bracelets and sets of handsome medals worn on the chest on a strap-work harness. The traditional mark of distinction in the Mediterranean world was a wreath of leaves worn on the head. Various types of wreaths were awarded to Roman soldiers and officers for special acts of courage, such as saving a comrade's life, or being first over the ramparts when attacking an enemy stronghold.

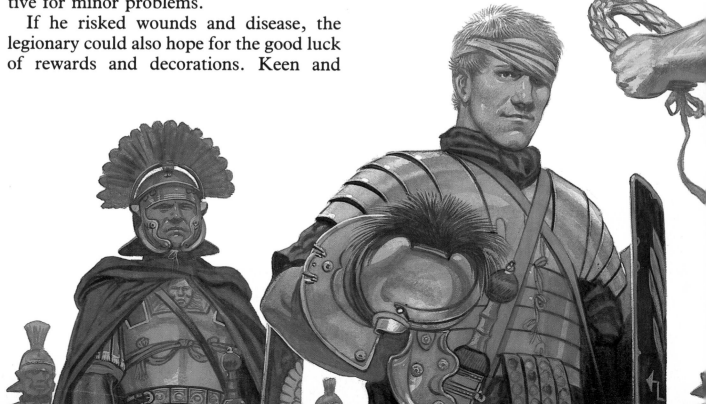

▽A legionary is awarded a wreath for bravery by his legion commander. The legion's eagle-bearer and most senior centurion stand nearby, while the unit parades in the background. Soldiers seem to have worn helmet crests only on ceremonial occasions. The sideways crests of centurions may have been worn in battle for quick identification of officers.

Soldiers at ease

Although his life was hard, the legionary did have some time to himself. The Romans loved steam-baths, and even the smallest forts usually had bath-houses where the tired soldiers could soak away their aches and pains and gossip and gamble with their comrades.

During peacetime duty in forts the Roman soldier enjoyed a varied diet. The army bread was made from wheat flour. Nuts, fruit, vegetables, eggs, milk and cheese were usually available. Meat rations could be beef, pork, mutton, goat, or game. Preserved fish was issued with a strong mackerel sauce, which must have livened up dull dishes. Romans loved oysters, and thousands of shells have been found on the sites of forts.

Most forts were close to towns or villages. In their free hours the soldiers visited the taverns and eating-houses, whose owners were happy to separate legionaries from their pay! Some soldiers even enjoyed a family life. They were forbidden to marry, but the rule was not strictly enforced, and it was not unusual for them to keep wives and children in nearby homes.

The legionary's pay was low, and deductions to pay for worn-out gear reduced it further. But part of it was always put aside for him as savings, and he occasionally got a large bonus to celebrate some important event. When he retired, he was given his savings and a discharge bonus of about ten years' pay. Old soldiers often lived fairly comfortably on land bought near their old fort, close to their friends.

▷ Off-duty soldiers enjoying themselves in a tavern. The bar counter, decorated with colored stone chips, has large built-in jars for hot wine, soup or food such as bean stew. Wine jars are racked in the background. Just like soldiers of all ages, Romans loved to gamble. Many dice have been found on military sites, as well as board games played with counters.

Glossary

Auxiliaries Lightly equipped troops recruited inside the Roman empire, but from men who did not have citizenship rights. When not supporting the legions in battle, the auxiliary cohorts manned frontier forts.

Barracks Permanent buildings inside a Roman fort in which the garrison lived. They were built either of timber or of plastered wicker panels on timber beams with a stone footing. The largest legionary bases were entirely stone-built.

Battering ram Heavy wooden beam with reinforced head, mounted to swing on ropes from a frame, and used to knock down enemy walls and gates.

Boss Domed metal reinforcement fixed in the middle of the outside surface of a shield to cover the hand grip on the inside.

Catapults The artillery of the Roman army: heavy spring-guns made like giant crossbows, which shot arrows and stones.

Centurion Roman army officer. Different grades of centurions commanded centuries and cohorts within the legion. They often transferred from legion to legion all over the empire.

Century A Roman army company of about 80 men. Six centuries made up a cohort.

Citizenship In the days of the Republic only Italians had full citizenship of Rome which brought political, legal and career privileges. Gradually the people who lived in other cities in the peaceful provinces of the empire were granted citizenship, which was also automatically given to time-expired auxiliary soldiers. In AD 212 the Emperor Caracalla granted citizenship to all men living in the empire who were not slaves.

Cohort A Roman army battalion of about 480 men. Ten cohorts made up a legion. At about the end of the 1st century AD this was reduced to eight normal cohorts and one double-strength 1st Cohort.

Eagle-bearer The officer in each legion who carried the eagle standard. Like other standard-bearers, he wore a fur pelt over his helmet and shoulders as a sign of rank.

Fatigues The daily duties and chores of a soldier's life around the fort.

Garrison The unit of soldiers assigned to live in a fort.

Legion A Roman army brigade of regular infantry, recruited only from citizens, and about 5,000 to 5,500 strong.

Legionary A private soldier of Roman regular infantry.

Mattock A digging tool, with a pick-axe blade on one side of the head and a spade blade on the other.

Standard The symbol of a military unit, usually carried on a pole, and regarded with great reverence.

Tortoise Roman troop formation, in which soldiers linked their shields around them and above their heads, making a protective "box" against enemy arrows and missiles.

Under the Roman Republic, before the first emperor, Augustus, came to the throne in 27 BC, Rome had already spread its power over Italy, Sicily, Spain, Greece, Yugoslavia, Tunisia, Libya, Turkey, Cyrenaica, Syria, Lebanon, France and the Low Countries. This took from 241 BC to 49 BC.

During the reign of **Augustus** (27 BC–AD 14) the empire embraced Egypt, the rest of Turkey, Palestine, Switzerland, Bavaria, parts of Austria and Hungary, Bulgaria, and part of West Germany.

AD 14–37	**Tiberius**
37–41	**Gaius (Caligula)**
41–54	**Claudius**
54–68	**Nero**
68–69	**Nero, Galba, Otho, Vitellius, Vespasian**
69–79	**Vespasian**
79–81	**Titus**
81–96	**Domitian**

During the years between the 40s and 80s AD, Morocco and England were added to the empire. There were also advances in West Germany.

96–98	**Nerva**
98–117	**Trajan**

Under the great soldier-emperor Trajan, the empire expanded to its greatest extent, taking in Jordan, Armenia, Assyria, Mesopotamia, and Rumania.

117–138	**Hadrian**
138–161	**Antoninus Pius**
161–180	**Marcus Aurelius**
180–193	**Commodus**
193	**Pertinax, Didius Julianus, Septimius Severus**
193–211	**Septimius Severus**

Index

PRINTED IN BELGIUM BY

proost
INTERNATIONAL BOOK PRODUCTION

3

DATE DUE

APR 9			
MAY 12			
MAR 1 ?			
2			
JAN 19			
APR 4			
GAYLORD			PRINTED IN U.S.A.